An Educational Coloring Book of DINOSAURS OF PREY

EDITOR
Linda Spizzirri

ILLUSTRATIONS
Peter M. Spizzirri

COVER ART
Peter M. Spizzirri

CONTENTS

OTHER LIZARD (Allosaurus) 2
TERRIBLE CLAW (Deinonychus) 4
BIRD ROBBER (Ornitholestes) 6
HORNED LIZARD (Ceratosaurus) 8
WOUNDING LIZARD (Dryptosaurus) 10
HOLLOW FORM (Coelophysis) 12
ALBERTA LIZARD (Albertosaurus) 14
TYRANT REPTILE (Tyrannosaurus) 16
GREAT LIZARD (Meglosaurus) 18
PRETTY JAW (Compsognathus) 20
MONSTER LIZARD (Teratosaurus) 22
THORN LIZARD (Spinosaurus) 24
CARCHARODON LIZARD (Carcharodontosaurus) 26
BIRD-LIKE LIZARD (Saurornithoides) 28
SLOW LIZARD (Segnosaurus) 30

Copyright, ©, 1985, 2005 by PETER M. SPIZZIRRI, All rights reserved.

An Educational Coloring Book of DINOSAURS OF PREY
Published by SPIZZIRRI PRESS, INC., P.O. BOX 9397, RAPID CITY, SOUTH DAKOTA 57709.
No part of this publication may be reproduced by any means without the express written consent of the publisher.
All national and international rights reserved on the entire contents of this publication.
Printed in the U.S.A.

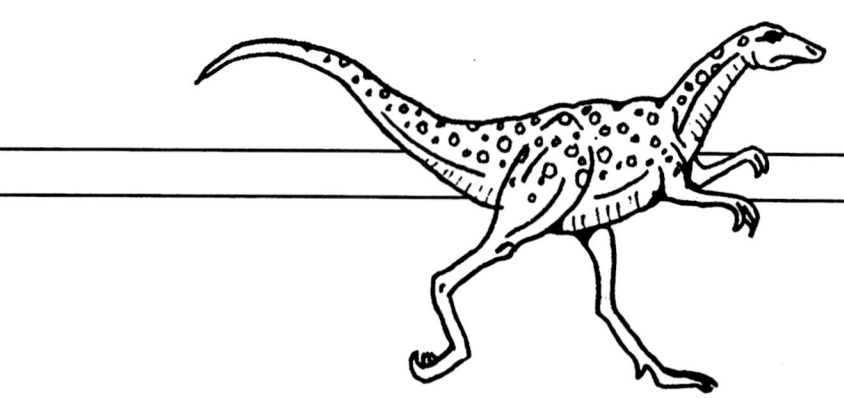

NAME:	OTHER LIZARD *(Allosaurus)*
WHERE IT IS FOUND:	NORTH AMERICA
SIZE:	UP TO 30 FEET LONG
WHEN IT LIVED:	JURASSIC TIME PERIOD 195 MILLION TO 140 MILLION YEARS AGO
WHERE IT LIVED:	FLOOD PLAINS, RIVER AND LAKE SHORES
WHAT IT MIGHT HAVE EATEN:	ANY PREY IT COULD CATCH AND KILL OR ANYTHING EATABLE IT COULD SCAVENGE
INTERESTING FACTS:	This giant carnosaur weighed up to 4 tons and was the most dangerous predator of the Jurassic period. Its powerful hind legs gave it great running speed plus the ability to leap long distances in pursuit of its prey. Because its jaws were equipped with large, pointed teeth and its forehands and feet had huge claws, its victims had little chance to escape once they were attacked.

ALLOSAURUS ATTACKING STEGOSAURUS

NAME:	TERRIBLE CLAW *(Deinonychus)*
WHERE IT IS FOUND:	UNITED STATES (WYOMING AND MONTANA)
SIZE:	8 FEET LONG
WHEN IT LIVED:	EARLY CRETACEOUS TIME PERIOD 140 MILLION TO 95 MILLION YEARS AGO
WHERE IT LIVED:	RIVER BANKS, WATERS' EDGE, FLOOD PLAINS
WHAT IT MIGHT HAVE EATEN:	ALL AVAILABLE LIFE FORMS, EVEN REPTILES MANY TIMES ITS SIZE
INTERESTING FACTS:	The discovery of the dromaesaurids made scientists aware that all dinosaurs were not slow-moving, stupid reptiles. These 150-pound flesh-eaters probably hunted in packs, like wolves of today. The pack hunting enabled them to prey on reptiles many times their size. *Deinonychus* had great speed and agility. A large brain enabled them to live less by instinct and made greater control over their body movements possible. *Deinonychus* was well equipped for hunting. It had dagger-sharp teeth and huge, gripping claws. Plus, the second toe on each foot had a 5-inch claw that was used for slashing kicks.

DEINONYCHUS PACK ATTACKING A TENONTOSAURUS

NAME:	BIRD ROBBER *(Ornitholestes)*
WHERE IT IS FOUND:	NORTH AMERICA (WYOMING)
SIZE:	6 FEET LONG
WHEN IT LIVED:	LATE JURASSIC TIME PERIOD 175 TO 140 MILLION YEARS AGO
WHERE IT LIVED:	RIVER BANKS AND FLOOD PLAINS
WHAT IT MIGHT HAVE EATEN:	SCAVENGER FOOD, INSECTS, MAMMALS, SMALL REPTILES
INTERESTING FACTS:	This 6-foot coelurosaur weighed only 70 pounds. Because it was relatively small among the giants of its day, it had to have great speed for hunting and to avoid being someone else's meal. Besides its speed, it was equipped with a long neck that enabled it to reach to the ground or leap into the air and catch its prey while running. *Ornitholestes* had three-fingered hands with large claws, enabling it to grasp its insect prey of 30-inch dragonflies or foot-long cockroaches.

ORNITHOLESTES CATCHING A DRAGONFLY

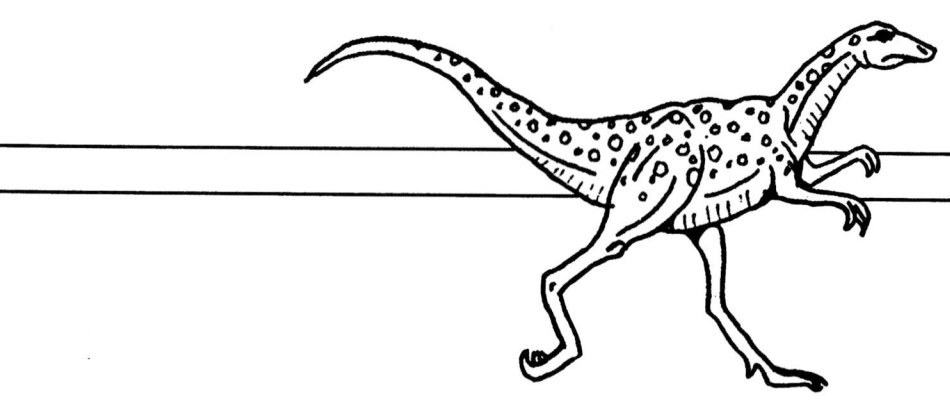

NAME:	HORNED LIZARD (*Ceratosaurus*)
WHERE IT IS FOUND:	UNITED STATES (COLORADO, UTAH, WYOMING)
SIZE:	15 TO 20 FEET LONG
WHEN IT LIVED:	UPPER JURASSIC TIME PERIOD 165 MILLION TO 140 MILLION YEARS AGO
WHERE IT LIVED:	FLOOD PLAINS AND ALONG SHORE LINES
WHAT IT MIGHT HAVE EATEN:	ALL AVAILABLE LIFE FORMS, EVEN REPTILES LARGER THAN ITSELF
INTERESTING FACTS:	This one to two-ton, flesh-eating giant had a unique horn on its nose. Horns are a weapon of defense and almost always are seen on plant eaters of the world. Because fossil footprints have been found in groups, it is supposed that they hunted in packs, like wolves of today. Pack hunting would have made the "horned lizard" capable of hunting very large prey.

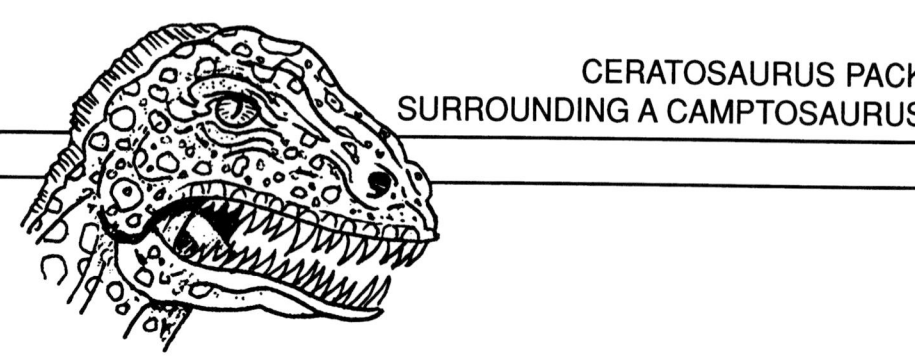

CERATOSAURUS PACK SURROUNDING A CAMPTOSAURUS

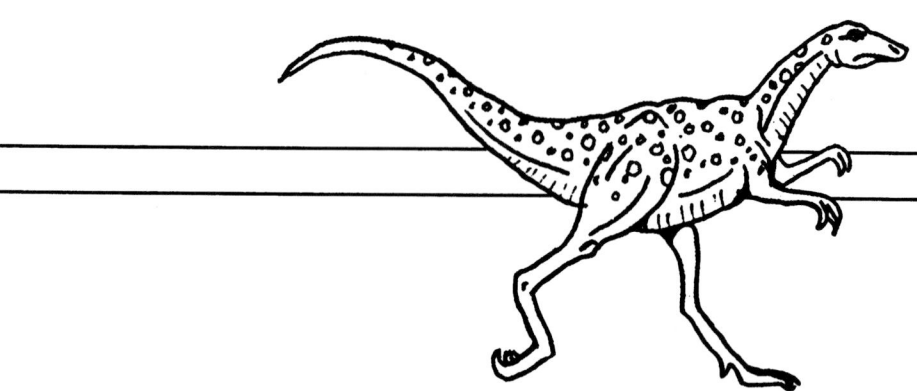

NAME:	WOUNDING LIZARD *(Dryptosaurus)*
WHERE IT IS FOUND:	NORTH AMERICA: COLORADO, WYOMING, MARYLAND, MONTANA, NEW JERSEY
SIZE:	OVER 20 FEET LONG
WHEN IT LIVED:	LATE CRETACEOUS TIME PERIOD 100 MILLION TO 63 MILLION YEARS AGO
WHERE IT LIVED:	DRY FLOOD PLAINS
WHAT IT MIGHT HAVE EATEN:	ANYTHING IT COULD CATCH OR SCAVENGE
INTERESTING FACTS:	This large, flesh-eating carnosaur had short, powerful arms and huge, muscular legs. It is theorized that it would leap along like a kangaroo, or take giant leaps to capture its prey. Because it was equipped with large, curved teeth and eagle-like claws on its hands and feet, *Dryptosaurus* could have been one of the most successful prehistoric hunters.

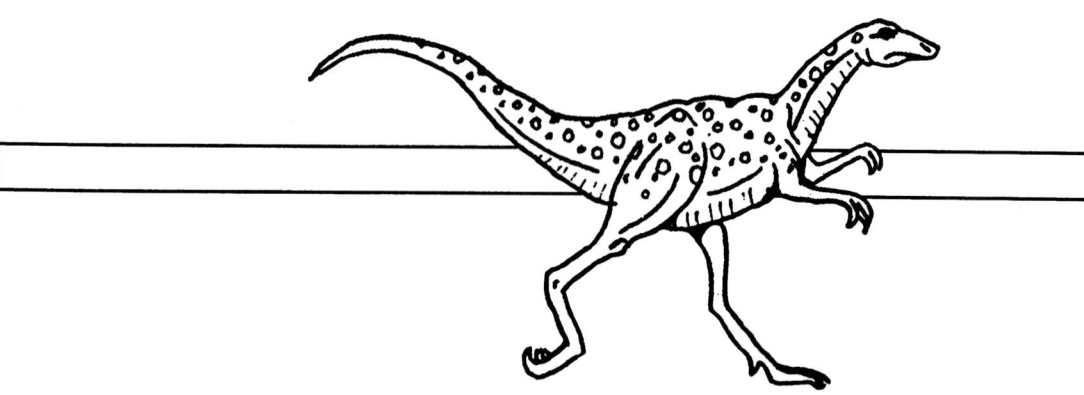

NAME:	HOLLOW FORM *(Coelophysis)*
WHERE IT IS FOUND:	EASTERN AND SOUTHWESTERN UNITED STATES
SIZE:	UP TO 10 FEET LONG
WHEN IT LIVED:	LATE TRIASSIC TIME PERIOD 215 MILLION TO 195 MILLION YEARS AGO
WHERE IT LIVED:	FLOOD PLAINS
WHAT IT MIGHT HAVE EATEN:	SCAVENGER FOOD, SMALL REPTILES AND AMPHIBIANS, OCCASIONALLY MAMMALS
INTERESTING FACTS:	Like the birds of today, the bones of this coelurosaur were hollow. That is how it got the name "hollow form." *Coelophysis* had many sharp, saw-edged teeth in its long, narrow jaw. Weighing between 50 and 60 pounds, it ran on bird-like legs and probably hunted game that was much smaller than itself.

COELOPHYSIS PURSUING AN ICAROSAURUS

NAME:	ALBERTA LIZARD *(Albertosaurus)*
WHERE IT IS FOUND:	MONTANA IN THE UNITED STATES AND ALBERTA, CANADA
SIZE:	26 FEET LONG
WHEN IT LIVED:	LATE CRETACEOUS TIME PERIOD 100 MILLION TO 63 MILLION YEARS AGO
WHERE IT LIVED:	FORESTS, FLOOD PLAINS
WHAT IT MIGHT HAVE EATEN:	SCAVENGER FOOD OR ANYTHING IT COULD CATCH, PREFERRED PLANT-EATING DINOSAURS
INTERESTING FACTS:	This 4000-pound dinosaur resembled *Tyrannosaurus* with its large head, but it had more teeth and a smaller body. It had tow-fingered arms that were weak and could not have been much use to *Albertosaurus*. Long, powerful legs that were equipped with huge, clawed toes, probably gave *Albertosaurus* the advantage of speed enabling it to run down and capture its prey.

ALBERTOSAURUS CHASING A LAMBEOSAURUS

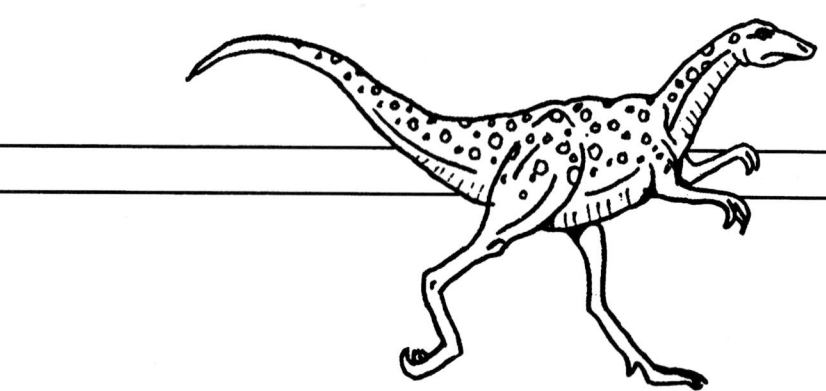

NAME:	TYRANT REPTILE *(Tyrannosaurus)*
WHERE IT IS FOUND:	NORTH AMERICA AND EAST ASIA
SIZE:	18 TO 20 FEET TALL, UP TO 50 FEET LONG
WHEN IT LIVED:	LATE CRETACEOUS TIME PERIOD 100 MILLION TO ABOUT 60 MILLION YEARS AGO
WHERE IT LIVED:	FOREST AND OPEN PLAINS
WHAT IT MIGHT HAVE EATEN:	SLOW-MOVING, ARMORED OR HORNED DINOSAURS, BUT PROBABLY FOUND MORE FOOD AS A SCAVENGER
INTERESTING FACTS:	*Tyrannosaurus* was probably the most powerful carnosaur to ever walk on earth. Its large head was more than 4-feet in length. Its huge jaw was filled with dagger-like teeth that were up to 6 inches in length. Regardless of their size, hunters and hunted alike must have been terrorized by the appearance of this 16,000-pound carnosaur.

TYRANNOSAURUS ATTACKING TRICERATOPS

NAME:	GREAT LIZARD *(Meglosaurus)*
WHERE IT IS FOUND:	ENGLAND AND EUROPE
SIZE:	20 TO 30 FEET LONG
WHEN IT LIVED:	JURASSIC TIME PERIOD 195 MILLION TO 140 MILLION YEARS AGO
WHERE IT LIVED:	FLOOD PLAINS, LAKE SHORES, AND FORESTS
WHAT IT MIGHT HAVE EATEN:	ANY PREY IT COULD FIND OR ANYTHING EATABLE IT COULD SCAVENGE
INTERESTING FACTS:	The first partial skeleton of this carnosaur was discovered in England, in 1824, and was only the second dinosaur "find" in recorded history. This first find consisted of some large bones and a lower jaw that had huge, sharp teeth. From these remains, Dean William Buckland (1784-1856), an English geologist, attempted the first written description of these giants. At that time, he thought *Meglosaurus* was more than 40-feet long. Further studies proved the correct size to be closer to 20 or 30 feet.

NAME:	PRETTY JAW *(Compsognathus)*
WHERE IT IS FOUND:	GERMANY AND FRANCE
SIZE:	2 FEET LONG (60 cm.)
WHEN IT LIVED:	LATE JURASSIC TIME PERIOD 160 MILLION TO 140 MILLION YEARS AGO
WHERE IT LIVED:	AREAS WITH UNDERGROWTH AND FORESTS
WHAT IT MIGHT HAVE EATEN:	LIZARDS, SMALL MAMMALS, INSECTS, AND SHELLFISH
INTERESTING FACTS:	*Compsognathus* has the distinction of being the smallest known dinosaur. It was about the size of a chicken. Its three-toed legs were twice as long as its two-fingered arms. It had a long tail for balance and a long neck which enabled it to catch prey while running. Living among the prehistoric giants, it had to have great speed and agility to hunt and survive. Bones of the swift-moving Jurassic lizard were found in the rib cage of one of its fossil remains.

COMPSOGNATHUS AND A HORSESHOE CRAB

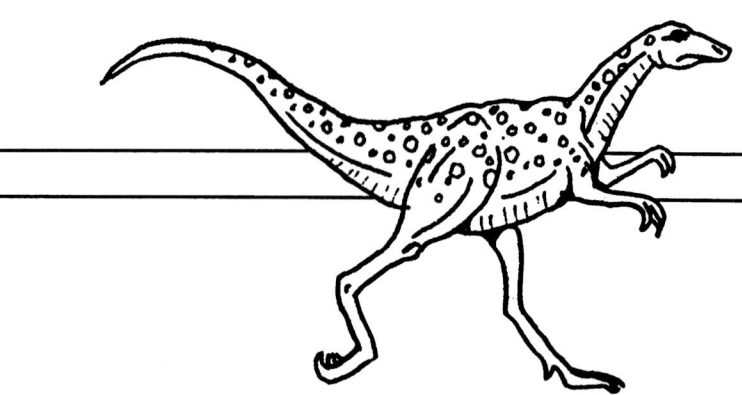

NAME:	MONSTER LIZARD (*Teratosaurus*)
WHERE IT IS FOUND:	GERMANY AND AFRICA
SIZE:	20 FEET LONG
WHEN IT LIVED:	LATE TRIASSIC TIME PERIOD 210 MILLION TO 195 MILLION YEARS AGO
WHERE IT LIVED:	DRY FLOOD PLAINS
WHAT IT MIGHT HAVE EATEN:	SCAVENGER FOOD OR ANY PREY IT COULD KILL
INTERESTING FACTS:	It is possible that the teratosaurids were one of the first families of flesh-eating, giant reptiles. The *Teratosaurus* weighed over 1000 pounds. It had an oversized head and a jaw filled with large, curved teeth. Its three-fingered hands were equipped with huge claws. Few fossil remains have been found, and there are those scientists who think teratosaurs may not have been dinosaurs at all.

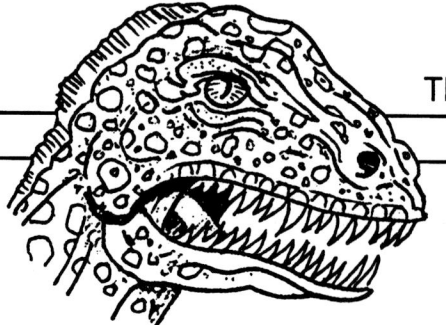

TERATOSAURUS WITH ITS PREY

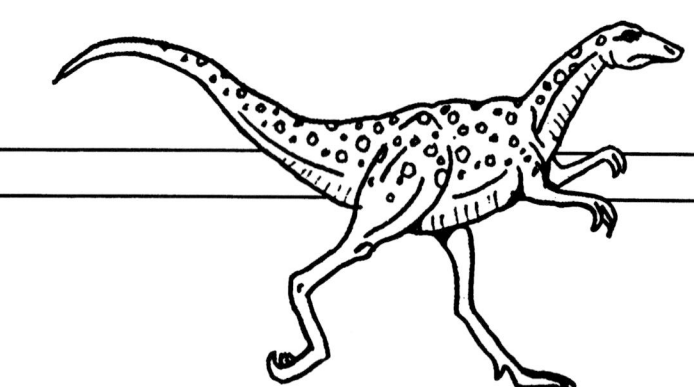

NAME:	THORN LIZARD *(Spinosaurus)*
WHERE IT IS FOUND:	EGYPT
SIZE:	30 FEET LONG
WHEN IT LIVED:	LATE CRETACEOUS TIME PERIOD 100 MILLION TO 60 MILLION YEARS AGO
WHERE IT LIVED:	WET FLOOD PLAINS
WHAT IT MIGHT HAVE EATEN:	SCAVENGER FOOD OR SLOW-MOVING HADROSAURS
INTERESTING FACTS:	This carnosaur had back spines that reached a length of 6 feet. These spines gave it the appearance of having a skin-sail mounted on its back. Scientists are not sure of how *Spinosaurus* used this skin-sail. Perhaps it was used to control its body heat. It might have been displayed so that *Spinosaurus* would look larger to its rivals or to threaten other predators.

NAME:	CARCHARODON LIZARD (*Carcharodontosaurus*)
WHERE IT IS FOUND:	SAHARA DESERT IN EGYPT
SIZE:	26 FEET LONG
WHEN IT LIVED:	EARLY CRETACEOUS TIME PERIOD 140 MILLION TO 95 MILLION YEARS AGO
WHERE IT LIVED:	FLOOD PLAINS
WHAT IT MIGHT HAVE EATEN:	ANY SLOW-MOVING PREY OR SCAVENGER FOOD
INTERESTING FACTS:	This megalosaurid was named carcharodon after the great white shark because of the large, saw-edged teeth that were in the jaw of its huge head. Like *Spinosaurus*, it is thought that the unusual high back vertebrae could have been used to control its body heat.

NAME:	BIRD-LIKE LIZARD *(Saurornithoides)*
WHERE IT IS FOUND:	MONGOLIA
SIZE:	6 1/2 FEET LONG
WHEN IT LIVED:	LATE CRETACEOUS TIME PERIOD 100 MILLION TO 63 MILLION YEARS AGO
WHERE IT LIVED:	FLOOD PLAINS, ALONG SHORES OF LAKES AND RIVERS, FORESTS
WHAT IT MIGHT HAVE EATEN:	SMALL REPTILES, MAMMALS, AND AMPHIBIANS
INTERESTING FACTS:	This bird-like dinosaur had a brain six times the size of a crocodile. This would have given it the ability to out-think other reptiles of that time. Its large eyes could focus to judge distance, just like people do. These large eyes probably made *Saurorinthoides* capable of hunting in the half-light of pre-dawn or dusk.

NAME:	SLOW LIZARD *(Segnosaurus)*
WHERE IT IS FOUND:	MONGOLIA AND EAST ASIA
SIZE:	13 FEET LONG
WHEN IT LIVED:	LATE CRETACEOUS TIME PERIOD 100 MILLION TO 63 MILLION YEARS AGO
WHERE IT LIVED:	NEAR WATER
WHAT IT MIGHT HAVE EATEN:	FISH, FROGS, TURTLES

INTERESTING FACTS: Tracks found near its fossil remains indicate *Segnosaurus* may have had webbed feet like a duck. Its long-nosed head had jaws with back teeth and a beak-tipped mouth. An unusual back-slanted hip bone probably made it difficult for it to move quickly on land. Scientists conclude that *Segnosaurus* was probably not a land hunter, but had more speed and agility in the water and would be more adept at hunting fish.

CATCHING FISH IN SHALLOW WATER

HOW TO DRAW "EASY LESSONS" BOOK TITLES

Cartoon Animals
Dinosaurs
Pets
Kids Drawing Book 1 & 2
Cartoon People
Animal Faces
People Faces
American Wildlife
Cartoon Faces

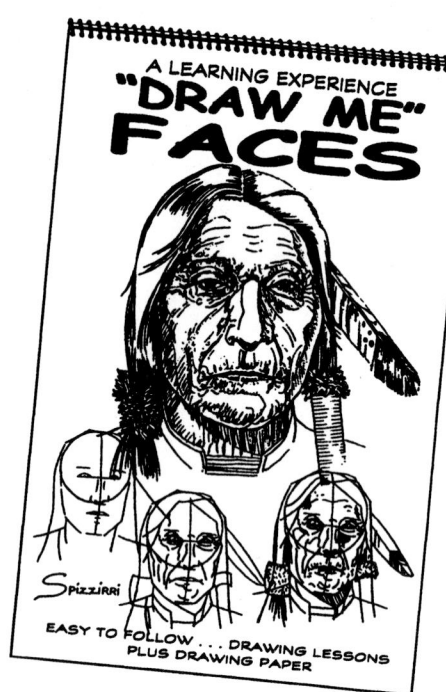

Drawing lessons for young children

8 1/2" x 11" and 11" x 17"
with drawing paper

9 Drawing Paper pads
in different sizes and paper weights

SPIZZIRRI PRESS, INC.
P.O. BOX 9397
RAPID CITY, SD 57709

PHONE: 1-800-325-9819
FAX: 1-800-322-9819
web: www.spizzirri.com
email: spizzpub@aol.com